Editor
Eric Migliaccio

Managing Editor
Ina Massler Levin, M.A.

Editor-in-Chief
Sharon Coan, M.S. Ed.

Illustrator
Sue Fullam

Cover Artist
Janet Chadwick

Art Coordinator
Kevin Barnes

Imaging
Rosa C. See

Product Manager
Phil Garcia

Publishers
Rachelle Cracchiolo, M.S. Ed.
Mary Dupuy Smith, M.S. Ed.

Punctuate & Capitalize

GRADE 4

Author

Susan Mackey Collins, M. Ed.

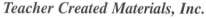

Teacher Created Materials, Inc.
6421 Industry Way
Westminster, CA 92683
www.teachercreated.com
ISBN-0-7439-3778-3
©2003 Teacher Created Materials, Inc.
Made in U.S.A.

Table of Contents

Introduction

The old adage "practice makes perfect" can really hold true for your child and his or her education. The more practice and exposure your child has with concepts being taught in school, the more success he or she is likely to find. For many parents, knowing how to help their children may be frustrating because the resources may not be readily available. As a parent, it is also difficult to know where to focus your efforts so that the extra practice your child receives at home supports what he or she is learning in school. This book has been written to help parents and teachers reinforce basic skills with children.

Practice Makes Perfect: Punctuate and Capitalize reviews basic grammar skills for fourth graders. The exercises in this book can be done sequentially or can be taken out of order, as needed.

The following standards or objectives will be met or reinforced by completing the practice pages included in this book. These standards and objectives are similar to the ones required by your state and school district and are appropriate for fourth graders.

- The student can identify and correctly use capital letters with dates, proper nouns (names and titles of people, names of towns, cities, counties, states, days of the week, months, streets, countries and holidays), and at the beginning of sentences.
- The student correctly capitalizes the heading, greeting and salutation of a friendly letter and the first word of a direct quotation.
- The student uses a colon between the hour and minutes when writing time.
- The student correctly uses periods with initials, abbreviations and certain titles before names.
- The student can identify declarative, interrogative and exclamatory sentences by recognizing the appropriate end mark.
- The student can correctly use an apostrophe to form possessives and contractions.
- The student uses commas correctly in a series; in dates and addresses; after certain introductory words; and in the heading, the greeting, and the closing of a friendly letter.
- The student correctly uses commas and quotation marks in writing dialog and correctly uses quotation marks in writing certain titles.

How to Make the Most of This Book

Here are some useful ideas for making the most of this book:

- Set up a certain time of day to work on these practice pages to establish consistency; or look for times in your day or week that are less hectic and more conducive to practicing skills.
- Keep all practice sessions with your child positive and constructive. If your child becomes frustrated or tense, set the book aside and look for another time to practice.
- Review the work your child has done.
- Pay attention to the areas in which your child has the most difficulty. Provide extra guidance and exercises in those areas.

Reference Guide

When working the exercises in this book, use this section as a reference guide.

Capitalize the first word at the beginning of a sentence:

→ The food at the picnic was so good, the ants took most of it with them.

Capitalize addresses:

→ 321 Powder Mill Drive
Ashland City, Tennessee 35467–1178

Capitalize names and dates:

→ December 28, 1966, is Carole Potter's birthday.

Capitalize titles of people:

→ Dr. Jones, Mrs. Smith, Captain Amis

Capitalize the names of towns, cities, counties, states, and countries:

→ She lives in Pleasant View in Cheatham County, which is located just north of Nashville, Tennessee.

→ I have traveled to Canada only once, but I would love to visit there again.

Capitalize days of the week, names of the months, and special holidays:

→ The newlyweds were married on a Saturday in February, right after Valentine's Day, but did not go on their honeymoon trip until after St. Patrick's Day.

Capitalize the heading, greeting, and salutation of a friendly letter:

→ 567 Grover Street
Primrose, AL 44457–9761

→ January 11, 2002

→ Dear Jane, Love you, Tommy

Capitalize the first word of a direct quotation:

→ Amanda asked, "Will you please pass the ketchup?"

Place a colon between the hour and the minutes:

→ 6:15, 12:00

Use a period with initials, abbreviations, and certain titles before names:

→ D.C., St., Mr., Dr.

Reference Guide *(cont.)*

Place a period at the end of a declarative sentence:

→ I like to eat liver and onions.

Place a question mark at the end of an interrogative sentence:

→ Do you like liver and onions?

Place an exclamation point at the end of an exclamatory sentence:

→ I can't believe you've never tried liver and onions!

Use an apostrophe to punctuate and form possessives and contractions:

→ That is Sadie's baby carriage.
→ The cats' dishes aren't filled with milk.

Use commas in a series:

→ I like country, jazz, and pop music.

Use commas in dates and addresses:

→ The ceremony will take place June 8, 2003, in Portland, Oregon.

Use commas in the heading, greeting, and closing of a friendly letter:

→ 64 Simons Avenue
Carter, CA 3245-8989
→ March 3, 2000
→ Dear Rhonda,
→ Yours always,

Use a comma after introductory words in a sentence:

→ Yes, I do want to go to the movies with you.

Use a comma in direct quotations:

→ Alicia said, "You are the nicest person I've ever met."

Use quotation marks correctly in writing dialog:

→ Simon asked, "Do you know where you put my surfboard?"
→ Tessa said, "I think I left it down on the beach."

Use quotation marks in writing certain titles:

→ The magazine article, "Get Up and Exercise," made me want to join a gym.

What a Way to Start

Capitalization Rule: Capitalize the first word at the beginning of a sentence.

Read the story below. If a word is capitalized incorrectly, draw an **X** on the letter that is not capitalized but should be. Then above the **X**, rewrite the word using correct capitalization.

my brother Jake and his friends were spending the night in a tent in our backyard. I wanted to join them, but Jake said I was too little and too scared to stay outside all night.

i wanted to prove who the real fraidy-cat was so I snuck outside and waited for my brother and his friends to go to sleep. When I heard snoring, I knew it was safe to slip inside the tent. I was about to put my pet frog inside my brother's sleeping bag when I heard something growl. I dropped my frog and ran screaming from the tent.

the noise of my screams woke-up everyone, and I had to confess what I had been about to do. when my brother's friends found out, they all had a good laugh. the growling was nothing more than my brother's friend, Tommy. apparently his stomach had been growling in protest all night long from eating too much junk food.

boy was I embarrassed!

Addressing Capitalization

Capitalization Rule: Capitalize words used in addresses.

Read each sentence below. Circle the capitalization errors in each address. Then rewrite each sentence correctly on the line provided.

1. My school is located at 27 maple Street.

   _____

2. I can't believe you went into the haunted house on scary avenue!

   _____

3. I told the florist to deliver the flowers to my home in river city, but instead he delivered them to a house in the town of dry creek.

   _____

   _____

4. Her aunt is sending her to stay at 111 caramel drive in chocolate town, New york.

   _____

   _____

5. I sent my letter to Santa Claus at rudolph Drive, snow city, North pole.

   _____

6. The advertisement stated I should send my check or money order to 857 Good deal street, Music Land, ohio.

   _____

   _____

7. Please send my bill to 2626 baptist Church road, adams, kentucky 34567-3456.

   _____

   _____

8. Do you live in Cedar Springs, kentucky?

   _____

9. The hospital is located on main Street in columbia, Arizona.

   _____

10. My mother was born in Cairo, georgia, but her sister was born in Texas.

   _____

   _____

The Right Name and Date

> **Capitalization Rule:** Capitalize proper nouns, such as the names of people and dates.

Look at the pictures below. On the line provided, write a first and last name to go with each picture. Be creative! Make up names like Crystal Ball or Jack O. Lantern.

1. _____

2. _____

3. _____

Write a sentence using each of the names you created. Be sure to include a date in your sentence. Remember to capitalize the names and the dates.

Example: Jack O. Lantern is going to a party on October 31.

1. _____

2. _____

3. _____

Write one more sentence using your own name and a date that is special to you.

_____

Capitalize Those Names and Dates

> **Capitalization Rule:** Capitalize proper nouns, such as the names of people and dates.

Complete each sentence with specific names and dates.

1. The person I admire the most is _____.

2. My birthday is _____.

3. The singer I listen to the most is _____.

4. The best teacher I ever had was _____.

5. If I had a pet tarantula, I would name it _____.

6. If I could chose my own first name, it would be _____.

7. A name that rhymes with Timmy is _____.

8. Valentine's Day is always the same date, _____.

9. This year we started school in the month of _____.

10. If I could choose, I would have us start school in the month of _____.

11. My favorite month of the year is _____.

12. In class, the person who sits beside me is named _____.

13. The name of my favorite actor or actress is _____.

14. Today's date is _____.

15. The person in charge of the school is named _____.

Quick Check #1

Read each sentence below. If the sentence is capitalized correctly, write **correct** on the line provided. If the sentence is capitalized incorrectly, rewrite the sentence and correct any capitalization errors.

1. My mother's full name is Alexandria gail maria wilson Smith.

   _____

2. My best friend, Amanda, gave me a basketball for my birthday.

   _____

3. Mom, can you tell me why uncle james has a hound dog named after him?

   _____

4. I once thought the president lived in white house, tennessee.

   _____

5. We drove to 112 lakeshore drive for my aunt's swimming party.

   _____

6. I can't believe you used to live at 2222 Tulane Street.

   _____

7. if I don't get at least eight hours of sleep, I'm as cranky as a bear.

   _____

8. When I go home, I'm going to watch television.

   _____

9. did you notice how beautiful the day was?

   _____

10. Before she got married her last name was smith, but now her last name is Zephelmacher.

   _____

10

Quick Check #2

Read the following letter. In the space provided, rewrite the letter using correct capitalization.

457 hopewood lane

cameron, AL 78943-2211

july 8, 2002

Dear nathan,

    I was so glad that you came to visit me. I wish melissa could have come, but I know she was busy at band camp. i hope she will come next time.

    we will probably be in our new house by next august. Our house is at 651 sunset drive, so be sure and write me at the new address.

    Tell bobby and irene that everyone here is thinking of them. they must be having such a wonderful time on their cruise! the only place I ever get to visit is the local zoo. oh well, it's better than nothing!

Love,

mark

_____

_____

_____

_____

_____

_____

_____

_____

_____

_____

Titles Aren't Just For Books

Capitalization Rule: Capitalize titles used with a person's name or in place of a person's name.

Look over the two columns. Choose a title in the first column and match it with a name in the second column. Rewrite a new title and name on each of the lines provided below. You may use a name more than once.

Column 1	**Column 2**
Doctor	Kitty
Coach	Lucille
Mr.	Candy
Mrs.	Smith
Miss	Sanders
Captain	Steve
Professor	Hatchet
Nurse	Kayla Beth
Mayor	Michael
Officer	Jones

1. _____

2. _____

3. _____

4. _____

5. _____

6. _____

7. _____

8. _____

9. _____

10. _____

Important Places

Capitalization Rule: Capitalize geographical names, such as the names of towns, cities, counties, states, and countries.

Pretend you have just been named king or queen of a small, relatively unknown country. Write the name of your new country on the line provided.

In the space below, draw an outline of your country. (Remember, it's your country, so it can be any shape.) Next, draw the borders for three states and three counties in your new country. Using correct capitalization, list the following geographical places on your map.

○ Using black ink, write the names of at least four towns or cities.

○ Using blue ink, write the names of three counties.

○ Using pencil, write the names of three states.

_____

(name of your country)

Time To Celebrate

Capitalization Rule: Capitalize days of the week, names of the months, and special holidays.

Look over the following calendar pages. Cross out any words not capitalized correctly and write them using correct capitalization.

February

sunday	Monday	Tuesday	wednesday	Thursday	friday	Saturday
			1 dentist appt.	2	3	4
5	6 band practice	7	8	9	10	11
12	13	14 valentine's Day	15	16	17 school dance	18
19	20	21	22 jack's birthday	23	24 soccer tryouts	25
26	27 boy scout's meeting	28				

Dear Me,

Capitalization Rule: Capitalize the heading, the greeting or salutation, and the closing of a friendly letter.

Circle all the capitalization errors in the friendly letters below.

9897 Blossom lane
peach City, ga 35467-1132
september 12, 2002

dear Ann,

Yesterday I had to go to the dentist. It was horrible. I had five cavities on each side of my mouth. The dentist said I would have to quit eating chocolate or my head would be full of nothing but fillings. I couldn't help but wonder why they couldn't all be chocolate fillings. Oh well! I will talk to you soon.

love always,

Carole

---

223 mockingbird street
allen, TN 38291-2777
october 9, 2003

Dear Aunt jane,

Hope all is well with you. Things were okay here until you left. We miss you so much. My friends came over yesterday to see you do some more of your lasso tricks, and I told them you had already left for the next rodeo.

Good luck on the circuit. I'll see you the next time you ride into town.

Sincerely,

sally mae

So You Said

Capitalization Rule: Capitalize the first word of a direct quote.

Read the following sentences. If the direct quotation is capitalized correctly, write **correct** on the line provided. If the sentence is not capitalized correctly, rewrite the sentence.

1. James said, "you are the meanest person I've ever met."

   _____

2. "Are you going to just sit there all day?" she asked.

   _____

3. Courtney replied, "someday I'm going to marry him."

   _____

4. The teacher said, "if you do not have your homework, you will not have recess."

   _____

5. The girl exclaimed, "I think you're wonderful!"

   _____

6. Chloe said, "you better not try to read my diary."

   _____

7. Scott asked, "Did you know you drool on your pillow every night when you fall asleep?"

   _____

   _____

8. Sandra exclaimed, "I don't want to go to the opera; I want to go shopping!"

   _____

   _____

9. "we are all going to campout on Halloween night," Drew explained.

   _____

10. "there will be no recess unless everyone sits down and gets quiet," Mrs. Norma stated.

    _____

Quick Check #3

Read the following letter. Next, go back and read over the words written in parentheses. Circle or highlight the answer choice that is capitalized correctly.

42 (dogwood, Dogwood) Street
(Hampton, hampton), VA 44444-1122
(december, December) 28, 2002

(Dear, dear) Lizzie,

On Christmas (day, Day) I finally got the new bicycle I wanted. It's the same one we saw last (saturday, Saturday) when we went to (davidson, Davidson) County to go shopping at the (Mall, mall). (Doctor, doctor) Brown, our neighbor, said it was the nicest bike he's seen in a long time. I like it because it's (blue, Blue), and everyone knows that's my favorite color.

I asked Mom if you could come back and visit for New (Year's, year's) Day, but she said, "(shelby, Shelby), you know Lizzie and her parents are traveling to (canada, Canada) for the remaining holidays." Actually, in the excitement over my new bicycle, I had forgotten all about your trip. I hope you have a (Wonderful, wonderful) time and be sure and tell (aunt, Aunt) Meredith to bring me back something special. She always buys the greatest gifts.

Hopefully, I will see you soon. Be sure and bring your bicycle the next time you come to visit. We can ride over to that burger place you like in (shakersville, Shakersville) and get something to eat.

(love, Love),

(shelby, Shelby)

Quick Check #4

Rewrite the following sentences, using capital letters as needed.

1. mr. and mrs. Boyte are good friends of my parents.

   _____

   _____

2. At the army base in kentucky, captain Jackson accepted only the best from his soldiers.

   _____

   _____

3. I live in cannon county in canton, Ohio.

   _____

   _____

4. My teacher, miss Lee, has had a pen pal from germany since she was in the third grade.

   _____

   _____

5. We have basketball practice every tuesday and thursday night during the months of november, December, and january; however, we don't have to practice on christmas Day.

   _____

   _____

6. coach Binkley said, "if you want to play, you've got to come to each and every practice."

   _____

   _____

7. When I get older, doctor Baldwin has promised me I can work at his veterinarian office in pleasant view.

   _____

   _____

8. Tristan asked, "Why do I have to clean my room every sunday?"

   _____

   _____

9. Cheatham County and hill County are the two counties left in the football tournament.

   _____

   _____

10. Monday, tuesday, wednesday, thursday, and Friday are the days we go to school.

    _____

    _____

It's Time

> **Punctuation Rule:** Use a colon between the hour and the minutes when you write the time.

Pretend you are keeping a journal of your daily activities. Write down the time you might begin each activity.

_____'s Daily Journal

- Wake-up   _____
- Make the bed   _____
- Get ready for school   _____
- Eat breakfast   _____
- Get to school   _____
- Morning announcements   _____
- English class   _____
- Math class   _____
- Lunch time   _____
- Go home   _____
- Watch television   _____
- Eat supper   _____
- Get ready for bed   _____
- Go to sleep   _____

Shorten It With a Period, Please

Punctuation Rule: Use a period with initials, abbreviations, and certain titles before names.

Read the list of words below. Use a period as needed to write the shortened form of each word or words.

1. street _____

2. Tennessee _____

3. mister _____

4. Mary Smith _____

5. doctor _____

6. avenue _____

7. Washington _____

8. Jay Jay _____

9. New York _____

10. United States of America _____

11. Cheatham Middle School _____

12. Friday _____

13. February _____

14. Adra Martin _____

15. District of Columbia _____

Make a Statement

> **Punctuation Rule:** A declarative sentence, a sentence that makes a statement, ends with a period.

Rewrite the following sentences, adding a period where needed.

1. I am twelve years old

   _____

2. My favorite colors are red, blue, and green

   _____

3. When the sun shines, everyone is happier

   _____

4. All the students went on the field trip

   _____

5. He had five overdue library books

   _____

Answer each question with a declarative sentence.

6. How old are you?

   _____

7. Do you like liver and onions?

   _____

8. What is your favorite school subject?

   _____

9. What is your favorite color?

   _____

10. If you could eat one food every day of the week, what would you eat?

    _____

Did You Know?

> **Punctuation Rule:** An interrogative sentence, a sentence that asks a question, ends with a question mark.

If you met someone from outer space, what are three questions you would ask?

1. _____
2. _____
3. _____

If you could ask your teacher three questions, what would you ask?

1. _____
2. _____
3. _____

If you could interview someone famous, what three questions would you ask?

1. _____
2. _____
3. _____

If you could talk to a ghost in a haunted house, what three questions would you ask it?

1. _____
2. _____
3. _____

It's So Exciting

Punctuation Rule: An exclamatory sentence, a sentence that shows excitement or emotion, ends with an exclamation point.

Read each set of sentences. None of the sentences contain ending punctuation marks. Add an exclamation point only to each exclamatory sentence.

1.
   A. My dog is a German shepherd
   B. That dog just bit me

2.
   A. How beautiful you look
   B. How do you get your hair so shiny

3.
   A. The house is on fire
   B. I wish you wouldn't burn my breakfast

4.
   A. There's a monster under my bed
   B. Mom says it's definitely time I cleaned up my room

5.
   A. When I get older, I'm going to be an astronaut
   B. How exciting it will be to travel in space

6.
   A. Did you see the movie that just came out
   B. I loved it

7.
   A. Homecoming will be fun
   B. I can't believe I get to be the queen

8.
   A. The traffic isn't moving very quickly
   B. There's a terrible wreck just ahead

9.
   A. How bright the full moon is
   B. Do you think any werewolves will be roaming the town

10.
   A. She changed her hair color from blonde to red
   B. She looks absolutely gorgeous

It's Mine...Or Maybe It's Yours

Punctuation Rules: Use an apostrophe to show ownership. An apostrophe is used to form the possessive case of a singular noun by adding an apostrophe and then the letter *s*.

Write a **C** on the line provided if the apostrophe is used correctly. Write an **X** if the apostrophe is used incorrectly.

_____ 1. dog's bone

_____ 2. deer's antlers

_____ 3. televisions' remote

_____ 4. womans' jacket

_____ 5. book's title

_____ 6. his' football

Change the following singular nouns to singular possessive nouns.

7. cat dish _____

8. dog treat _____

9. teacher desk _____

10. Kayla Beth doll _____

11. horse oats _____

Read over the list of objects. Using an apostrophe, give each object a singular owner.

Example: guitar _____the musician's guitar_____

12. banjo _____

13. pizza _____

14. notebook _____

15. money _____

The Important Apostrophe

Punctuation Rules: Use an apostrophe to show ownership. For plural nouns not ending in *s*, add an apostrophe and an *s*. For plural nouns ending in *s* add only an apostrophe.

Write the plural possessive of the following words.

Plural   **Plural Possessive**

1. dogs   _____

2. kids   _____

3. children   _____

4. deer   _____

5. women   _____

6. toys   _____

7. geese   _____

8. hats   _____

9. sisters   _____

10. movies   _____

In the space below, choose any five of the ten plural possessive words listed above and use them each in a sentence.

1. _____

_____

2. _____

_____

3. _____

_____

4. _____

_____

5. _____

_____

When Two Become One

> **Punctuation Rule:** Use an apostrophe to form a contraction.

Look over the following lists. On the line provided, write the letter of the contraction from List 2 that is correct for each group of words in List 1.

List 1	List 2
_____ 1. were not	A. isn't
_____ 2. does not	B. hasn't
_____ 3. should not	C. weren't
_____ 4. I am	D. doesn't
_____ 5. let us	E. they're
_____ 6. was not	F. shouldn't
_____ 7. is not	G. wasn't
_____ 8. they are	H. let's
_____ 9. has not	I. you're
_____ 10. you are	J. I'm

Write the correct set of words for the following contractions.

1. don't   _____

2. haven't   _____

3. hadn't   _____

4. wouldn't   _____

5. she'd   _____

Quick Check #5

Rewrite the following sentences. Add colons, periods, question marks, exclamation marks, and apostrophes where needed.

1. At 1200 midnight the young girl lost her glass slipper _____

2. How quickly the time flew _____

3. Was there ever a girl more beautiful than she was on that magical, fairy tale night

4. Why didnt she remember to get home before 1200 in the morning _____

5. The girls carriage turned into a pumpkin _____

6. How lovely everything was before the magic disappeared _____

7. Little girls everywhere dream of living in the princes castle. _____

8. The girl cant be the princes bride, unless her feet fit the glass slipper

9. Lifes like a fairy tale; there are good days and there are bad days. _____

10. Just remember, if you go to a ball, wear a watch that keeps perfect time _____

Quick Check #6

Read each sentence. Circle the letter of the sentence that is punctuated and written correctly.

1.

   A. My little sister was born at 6:05 in the morning.

   B. My little sister was born at 605 in the morning.

2.

   A. Mr. Carter is my science teacher at C.M.S.

   B. Mr Carter is my science teacher at C.M S.

3.

   A. Of course Ill marry you?

   B. Of course I'll marry you!

4.

   A. I couldn't eat a grasshopper.

   B. I couldnt eat a grasshopper.

5.

   A. Allisons cat is named Stinkerbell.

   B. Allison's cat is named Stinkerbell.

6.

   A. Your new house on Oak St. is just fabulous!

   B. Your new house on Oak St is just fabulous!

7.

   A. In the army, K.P. stands for kitchen patrol, but my friend Kristen Phillips' initials are also K.P.

   B. In the army, K.P. stands for kitchen patrol, but my friend Kristen Phillips initials are also K P.

8.

   A. Isnt your appointment with Dr Smith at 12 00 noon!

   B. Isn't your appointment with Dr. Smith at 12:00 noon?

9.

   A. I won't do it!

   B. I want do it?

10.

   A. Derek's little sisters are much nicer than he is.

   B. Dereks little sister's are much nicer than he is.

Separate, Separate, Separate

> **Punctuation Rule:** Use commas to separate items in a series.

Complete the following sentences. Be sure to insert commas as needed.

1. My favorite hobbies are _____

   _____ and _____.

2. Some of my favorite people are _____

   _____ and _____.

3. Three places I would like to visit are _____

   _____ and _____.

4. Three places I have visited are _____

   _____ and _____.

5. My least favorite foods are _____

   _____ and _____.

Read the following sentences. Insert commas as needed.

1. I need to buy milk bread and eggs.

2. My favorite seasons are spring winter and fall.

3. She is nice sweet and kind to everyone she meets.

4. I read ate and slept during the long drive.

5. Do you like Jennifer Karen Olivia or Michele the best?

Use commas to separate items in a geographical lists.

1. List three oceans: _____

2. List three mountain ranges: _____

3. List three rivers: _____

4. List four countries: _____

5. List three continents: _____

A Great Date

Punctuation Rule: Use a comma to separate the day and the year when writing a date.

Some months have thirty days; others have thirty-one. One month even has twenty-eight days and sometimes twenty-nine, but every month has a first day.

On the lines provided list the twelve months of the year and write the date on each line as if it is the first day of the month. Write the current year to complete the date.

1. January 1, 2003 _____

2. _____

3. _____

4. _____

5. _____

6. _____

7. _____

8. _____

9. _____

10. _____

11. _____

12. _____

Add commas as needed to the following dates:

13. July 4 1776

14. April 26 1955

15. December 28 1966

16. July 20 1969

17. March 17 2003

18. May 15 1981

What's Your Address?

> **Punctuation Rule:** Use a comma to separate items in an address such as the street, the city, and the state. Do not place a comma between the state and the zip code.

It's time to go on an address treasure hunt. Before you begin you will need the following books: a telephone book, any school textbook, and a library book.

1. Look inside your grammar book or any of your schoolbooks. Write the publisher's address.

   _____

   _____

2. Look in the business directory of the phone book and find an address for any business listed. Write the name of the business and the address.

   _____

   _____

3. Pretend you live at 3666 Covington Lane in Chicago, Illinois, and your zip code is 89987–1234. Now, write your new address.

   _____

   _____

4. Look inside a library book and write down the address of the publisher.

   _____

   _____

5. Use a phonebook to find the address of someone whose last name starts with the letter M. Write this person's address.

   _____

   _____

Read through the following addresses. Add commas wherever they are needed.

6. 342 Meadow View Lane Sommerset MA 78965–3221

7. P.O. Box 53 Springfield Tennessee

8. Dallas Texas 75526–1234

9. 700 Scoutview Drive Ashland Georgia

10. Fairbanks Alaska

The Friendly Comma

> **Punctuation Rule:** Use commas in the heading, greeting or salutation, and closing of a friendly letter.

Read the following friendly letter. Insert commas as needed.

88 Westmoreland Drive

Darlington Maine 78912–0987

January 12 2002

Dear June

    How have you been? The last time you were here, we were having some very bad luck. The well was frozen, and we didn't have any water. It was hard going for three weeks without a bath, but it was even harder not to be able to brush our teeth. I was sorry to hear you had three cavities when you got back home and went to see your dentist.

    Things are better now. At least we have running water again. I'm not too sure when we'll get our electricity back. A construction truck ran into our electrical pole last week and then the blizzard came so no one could get out to fix the lines. Of course, we'd have probably lost the electricity anyway, because of the five feet of snow. I just hope I can shovel my way out the door and get this letter to the mailbox.

    I will talk to you soon. Take care and stay warm.

Always

Jack Frost

The Friendly Comma *(cont.)*

Read the following friendly letter. Insert commas as needed.

P.O. Box 358

Richville Oregon 98761–0223

November 17 2003

Dear Sasha

    I have been trying to reach you for days, but your phone must not be working. Daddy says you have to come back and get your cat. Our poor poodle has started hiding under the bed since Whiskers came to stay with us. He is terrified of her and won't come out, even for his favorite snack. I fear if you don't come and get her soon, Daddy will send her back to you in her pet crate, and she so dislikes going anywhere in her crate. Please come as soon as you get this letter. I like Whiskers, but I do miss seeing my poodle every day.

See you soon

Lori

Add commas as needed to the items below.

1. December 15 1999

2. Dear Mark

3. Love you a bunch

4. Sincerely

5. 345 Oaklawn Drive
   Camelot CA 34571-6767
   July 18, 2002

Introducing With a Comma

Punctuation Rule: Use a comma after certain introductory words in a sentence such as yes, well, no, or why.

Complete the following statements. Be sure and use a comma after each introductory word.

1. No I don't like _____.

2. Yes I have been to _____.

3. Well I guess my favorite movie is _____.

4. Why it's my best friend _____!

5. Well I think you are _____.

6. Yes you can have my _____.

7. No I don't want to go to _____.

8. Why I can't believe you think _____!

9. Yes chocolate is definitely better than _____.

10. No I will never, ever _____.

Mix and Match: Choose an introductory word from column A and match it with a group of words from column B. Write the new sentence on the line provided.

A	B
No	some frogs are princes in disguise
Well	I don't want any frog legs for supper
Yes	most frogs taste just like chicken
Why	I've heard frogs can cause warts

11. _____

_____

12. _____

_____

13. _____

_____

14. _____

_____

Quick Check #7

Insert commas to punctuate correctly.

1. My favorite meals are breakfast lunch and supper.

2. We will attend the meeting at 372 Anderson Lane Smithville Kentucky.

3. Yes you do look like someone I once knew.

4. Well I would like to go hiking fishing and camping.

5. My grandmother is from Nashville Tennessee.

6. Dear Robert

    Please don't be mad at me. I broke the handle bars on your new bicycle. I will use my allowance to have them repaired. The good news is I only had to get five stitches. The bad news is we can't fix your bike with just a few stitches.

    I'm really sorry.

    Sincerely

    Irene

7. Please deliver the package to 1789 Grover Drive Barsdale Oregon 34567–1299.

8. I wish I could take a nap and sleep sleep and sleep some more.

9. Yes I do like ice-cream sodas.

10. Why I never guessed you liked her!

11. The package was addressed to 85 North Michigan Avenue Louisville Kentucky but was delivered to 85 South Michigan Avenue.

12. Well the last time I saw him he was only three inches tall.

13. Why performing a play about the world's greatest inventors is a great idea for the drama club the science club and the entire school!

14. Dear Sandra

    Please send me the money you owe me. Cash works nicely, but I will also take a check.

    Sincerely

    Teresa

15. You are nice pretty and kind.

16. No I would never tell a lie.

17. Kevin made failing grades on his science social studies and math tests.

18. She has taught first grade second grade and third grade.

19. Well that is the funniest thing I've ever seen.

20. No I won't share my popsicle with you.

Quick Check #8

Read the envelope and letter below. Add commas wherever needed.

Dewanna Phillips

347 Kingston Place

Benson Louisiana 60976–3251

        Betty Boyte

        P.O. Box 78

        Brigham Louisiana 60986–1231

---

        347 Kingston Place

        Benson Louisiana 60976–3251

        December 23 2002

Dear Betty

    I wanted to write and wish you a happy holiday. I wish we would have snow over the school break, but since it's hot enough to go swimming, I doubt that will happen. Why it's hot enough outside to fry an egg on the sidewalk!

    Did you ask your parents for anything special for Christmas? I asked for a camera some film and a gerbil. Well I doubt I'll get the gerbil, but it never hurts to ask.

    I will talk to you not Monday Tuesday or Wednesday because we will be gone for the fishing trip, but I will definitely call you on Thursday.

        Stay cool

        Dewanna

Hey, You!

> **Punctuation Rule:** Use a comma to separate a direct quotation from the rest of the sentence.

Read the following sentences. Insert commas wherever needed.

1. Jack said "Yesterday I went to the dentist."

2. "I hate going to the dentist" Marie responded.

3. "It wasn't too bad. I only had one cavity" Jack replied.

4. "Well, when I go, I hope I don't have any cavities" Marie said.

5. Jack answered "If you brush your teeth regularly you probably won't have any cavities."

6. Marie said "Of course I brush regularly. I use my favorite toothbrush."

7. Jack responded "I can't believe you have a favorite toothbrush. What is it?"

8. Marie answered shyly "Oh, it's nothing. Never mind."

9. Jack said "You have to tell me what it is. You've made me curious."

10. "Good grief! If you must know, it's a toothbrush shaped like an elephant. I use the long trunk that's filled with bristles to reach my back teeth, and the bristles on the tusks clean my front teeth. That's why my teeth are always pearly white" Marie explained.

You Said What?

Punctuation Rule: Use quotation marks in writing dialog or conversation. Quotation marks enclose a person's exact words.

Read the following conversation. Add quotation marks wherever needed. Quotation marks already included are correct.

"I get to go to the concert next week! Christie exclaimed.

How did you get tickets?" Brandon asked.

I won them from a contest on the radio, Christie explained.

"You have to be the luckiest person I've ever met," Brandon said.

"Yes, I am, Christie said with a smile.

Brandon asked, "How many tickets did you win?

Two," replied Christie.

"Have you decided who is going with you? Brandon asked innocently.

"Whoever I invite will have to be someone who is very nice to me," Christie said.

"Of course," Brandon agreed. "By the way, Christie, do you need any help with your homework?

"Nice try, Brandon, Christie said.

"What? Brandon asked innocently.

"I was going to invite you anyway, Christie said.

Thank goodness," Brandon replied. "I don't even have my own homework finished yet. I didn't know how I was going to help you with yours!"

Titles, Titles, and More Titles

Punctuation Rule: Use quotation marks in writing titles of short works such as magazine articles, short stories, poems, songs, and chapters of books.

Read each description below. On the line provided, create a title for each description that is given. Be sure and place quotation marks around the title.

1. Write a country song title about a man who is having a hard time with his animals. His dog has only three legs. His favorite chicken is missing, and his horse ran away from the farm.

   _____

2. Write a chapter title for a book _The Spookiest Night_. In the chapter some teenage kids are daring each other to spend the night in the haunted house. The house is said to be haunted by three poltergeists.

   _____

3. Write a title for a poem about a beautiful, spring day.

   _____

4. Write a title for a magazine article about a boy who really did have ants in his pants.

   _____

5. Write a title for a short story about a boy and his very first pet, a snake named Hank.

   _____

Go to the library or look at your house and find a book where the chapters have titles. Write down the titles of the first five chapters. A reminder: book titles are underlined or italicized; chapter titles are placed in quotation marks.

Title of the book: _____

Chapter one: _____

Chapter two: _____

Chapter three: _____

Chapter four: _____

Chapter five: _____

Quick Check #9

Correct the following sentences by adding commas or quotation marks where needed.

1. Steve said "I want to build a tree house."

2. "Where will you build it? Sandra asked.

3. "I want to build it in the maple tree in my yard" Steve explained.

4. Can I help you?" Sandra asked.

5. "Of course you can, but I get to make all the decisions. You are just the helper, Steve said.

6. Well, if that's the case, I think I'll just build my own tree house," Sandra answered.

7. "Wait!" Steve exclaimed. "I've changed my mind. You can help make some of the decisions.

8. "You're only saying that because my daddy owns a lumber mill, and you know I can get the wood" Sandra said.

9. "I do need wood to build my tree house, Steve admitted.

10. I'll help you," Sandra finally said, "but only if you call me Queen Sandra for the rest of the day.

11. "Good grief! Steve complained.

12. Take it or leave it," Sandra responded.

13. "Okay. Okay," Steve agreed. "Let's go build that tree house now, Queen Sandra.

14. "You don't have to bow down when you call me that, Sandra said.

15. "Trust me; I wasn't," Steve said. "I was just tying my shoelace.

Each of the following titles belongs to a short work such as a poem, song, or article. Rewrite each title using quotation marks.

16. A Wonderful Day _____

17. You Are My Life _____

18. The Cat With Three Whiskers _____

19. My Goat, Gabrielle _____

20. The Day No Dogs Would Howl_____

Quick Check #10

Finish the following quotations. Use commas and quotation marks where needed.

1. Kenneth said _____.

2. _____ said Tammy.

3. Angie argued, "There is no way I'm going to let you _____.

4. "I wouldn't go with you even if you were _____, Sandy said.

5. Janie explained _____.

Read the following sentences. Place quotation marks around the titles of short works.

6. The chapter I like best is Swimming, Swimming, Swimming, in the book <u>Summer Vacation</u>.

7. She Can Wait is my favorite song.

8. I read the article, Getting Better Grades, but I still made a D on the test.

9. My father wrote the hit song, Daddy Is Great, but he says the words are about his own father.

10. In <u>Teenager Magazine</u>, the article Communicating With Parents really helped me communicate with my own family.

Read the following sentences. Add quotation marks where needed.

11. Snow days are the best school days, Jack said.

12. I agree with you, Sarah replied.

13. Jack responded, I wish we could get a snow day soon.

14. Sarah answered, You know that will never happen. The temperature today reached over one hundred degrees!

15. Jack sighed and said, I think I'm going to move to the North Pole.

Unit Assessment

Shade in the bubble of the sentence that is written correctly.

1. (a) i don't like spinach.
   (b) she can't wait to go to the races.
   (c) He is my brother.

2. (a) My best friend is Sandy Jones.
   (b) yesterday was my birthday.
   (c) all the children are taking a nap.

3. (a) She lives on Oaklawn drive.
   (b) My parents own a house on chestnut Avenue.
   (c) I sent the letter to 376 Smith Drive.

4. (a) My uncle lives in Lexington, Kentucky.
   (b) The address she gave me was 101 Willow street.
   (c) If you come to smallville, please stop by and see me.

5. (a) Did you give stephanie the ball?
   (b) I think Adam is so nice.
   (c) I thought I saw erica at the store.

6. (a) tom, please come here.
   (b) Matthew takes karate lessons.
   (c) Tell chloe to tie her shoes.

7. (a) Doctor, can we see him now?
   (b) My doctor's name is doctor Hampton.
   (c) I have an interview with mayor Thompson.

8. (a) Officer jones caught the thief.
   (b) In English class Mrs. Smith assigned a book report.
   (c) Nurse valorie gave her the vaccine.

9. (a) We have a vacation house in Gatlin, wyoming.
   (b) She moved from Caroll County to cannon County.
   (c) She visited Paris, France on her tour.

10. (a) We moved to Sandy Springs from Thomasville.
    (b) I have never been to mexico.
    (c) North america is not a country.

Unit Assessment *(cont.)*

Shade in the bubble that completes the sentence or group of words correctly.

11. **My favorite month is _____.**
    - ⓐ february
    - ⓑ feb.
    - ⓒ February

12. **_____ is the first day of the week.**
    - ⓐ sunday
    - ⓑ Sunday
    - ⓒ Friday

13. **We eat turkey for _____ dinner.**
    - ⓐ thanksgiving
    - ⓑ ThanksGiving
    - ⓒ Thanksgiving

14. **Dear _____**
    - ⓐ Jack;
    - ⓑ Jack,
    - ⓒ Jack!

15. **Love _____**
    - ⓐ always,
    - ⓑ Always
    - ⓒ always!

16. **The address on the letter was 86 _____.**
    - ⓐ Cumberland Street
    - ⓑ cumberland Street
    - ⓒ Cumberland street

17. **Her return address was in Summerset, _____.**
    - ⓐ georgia
    - ⓑ Utah
    - ⓒ tenn.

18. **She wrote the letter _____ 10, 1988.**
    - ⓐ may
    - ⓑ june
    - ⓒ December

19. **Terrell said, "_____ like hot wings and hot sauce."**
    - ⓐ me
    - ⓑ i
    - ⓒ I

20. **"_____, do you think math is fun?" Alicia asked.**
    - ⓐ ken
    - ⓑ Robert
    - ⓒ simon

21. **My lunch begins at _____ noon.**
    - ⓐ 12:00
    - ⓑ 12;00
    - ⓒ 12,00

22. **I live at 153 Boker _____.**
    - ⓐ avenue
    - ⓑ street
    - ⓒ Ave.

23. **My teacher, _____ Handy, is very nice.**
    - ⓐ mrs.
    - ⓑ Mrs;
    - ⓒ Mrs.

24. **The house is on fire _____**
    - ⓐ ?
    - ⓑ !
    - ⓒ .

25. **How do we get there from here**
    - ⓐ .
    - ⓑ !
    - ⓒ ?

26. **I have to go to class _____**
    - ⓐ !
    - ⓑ ?
    - ⓒ .

27. **She is a good friend _____**
    - ⓐ .
    - ⓑ ?
    - ⓒ !

Unit Assessment *(cont.)*

Shade in the bubble that completes the sentence or group of words correctly.

28. Where did you put your _____ gift?
- (a) Mothers
- (b) Mothers'
- (c) Mother's

29. The _____ jackets are hanging in the closet.
- (a) boys'
- (b) boys
- (c) boy's

30. I _____ know what _____ talking about!
- (a) don't, you're
- (b) don't, your
- (c) don't, you're

Shade in the bubble of the sentence showing the correct punctuation.

31.
- (a) I will eat fish chocolate and corn.
- (b) I will eat, fish, chocolate, and corn.
- (c) I will eat fish, chocolate, and corn.

32.
- (a) My grandmother's birthday is July 1; 1945.
- (b) My grandmother's birthday is July 1, 1945.
- (c) My grandmother's birthday is July 1 1945.

33.
- (a) The party was at 32 Main Street, Sango Maine.
- (b) The party was at, 32 Main Street, Sango, Maine.
- (c) The party was at 32 Main Street, Sango, Maine.

34.
- (a) Yes I want to go with you.
- (b) Yes; I want to go with you.
- (c) Yes, I want to go with you.

35.
- (a) Carole said, "Your brownies are delicious."
- (b) Carole said "Your brownies are delicious."
- (c) Carole said: "Your brownies are delicious."

36.
- (a) Tara stated, "I don't know how to work the copier."
- (b) Tara stated, I don't know how to work the copier."
- (c) Tara stated, I don't know how to work the copier.

37.
- (a) My favorite poem, Spiders Spinning, is very funny.
- (b) My favorite poem, Spiders Spinning, is very funny.
- (c) My favorite poem, "Spiders Spinning," is very funny.

Unit Assessment *(cont.)*

Read the following letters. Shade in the bubble that shows correct punctuation for the heading, greeting or salutation, and closing of a friendly letter.

---

834 Sykes Drive
Banks North Carolina 89032-1124
January 8 2003

Dear Cade

    I really enjoyed coming to your house for the weekend. I hope you will be able to visit me soon. We can go to the amusement park.

Your friend

Jake

---

38. The salutation should be as follows:

  (a) Dear, Cade   (b) Dear Cade,   (c) Dear Cade:

39. In the heading there should be a comma between

  (a) the city and state   (b) the state and zip code (c) no commas needed

40. The correct closing would be as follows:

  (a) Your friend, Jake   (b) Your, friend   (c) Your friend,

---

1245 Elliot Street
Hamilton CA 32198-0909
December 11 2003

Dear Brandi

    Can you come to my house next Friday? I haven't seen you in over a month. When you come, please bring back all of the things you borrowed from me.

See you soon

Brittani

---

41. The salutation should be as follows:

  (a) Dear, Brandi,   (b) Dear, Brandi: (c) Dear Brandi,

42. In the heading there should be no comma between

  (a) the state and the zip code

  (b) the city and the state

  (c) the day of the month and the year

43. The closing should be written as

  (a) See You Soon!   (b) See you soon: (c) See you soon,

Answer Key

Page 6

My brother Jake and his friends were spending the night in a tent in our backyard. I wanted to join them, but Jake said I was too little and too scared to stay outside all night.

I wanted to prove who the real fraidy-cat was so I snuck outside and waited for my brother and his friends to go to sleep. When I heard snoring, I knew it was safe to slip inside the tent. I was about to put my pet frog inside my brother's sleeping bag when I heard something growl. I dropped my frog and ran screaming from the tent.

The noise of my screams woke-up everyone, and I had to confess what I had been about to do. When my brother's friends found out, they all had a good laugh. The growling was nothing more than my brother's friend, Tommy. Apparently his stomach had been growling in protest all night from eating too much junk food.

Boy was I embarrassed!

Page 7

1. My school is located at 27 Maple Street.
2. I can't believe you went into the haunted house on Scary Avenue.
3. I told the florist to deliver the flowers to my home in River City, but instead he delivered them to a house in the town of Dry Creek.
4. Her aunt is sending her to stay at 111 Caramel Drive in Chocolate Town, New York.
5. I sent my letter to Santa Claus at Rudolph Drive, Snow City, North Pole.
6. The advertisement stated I should send my check or money order to 857 Good Deal Street, Music Land, Ohio.
7. Please send my bill to 2626 Baptist Church Road, Adams, Kentucky 34567-3456.
8. Do you live in Cedar Springs, Kentucky?
9. The hospital is located on Main Street in Columbia, Arizona.
10. My mother was born in Cairo, Georgia, but her sister was born in Texas.

Page 8 and 9

Answers will vary.

Page 10

1. My mother's full name is Alexandria Gail Maria Wilson Smith.
2. Correct
3. Mom, can you tell me why Uncle James has a hound dog named after him?
4. I once thought the president lived in White House, Tennessee.
5. We drove to 112 Lakeshore Drive for my aunt's swimming party.
6. Correct
7. If I don't get at least eight hours of sleep, I'm as cranky as a bear.
8. Correct
9. Did you notice how beautiful the day was?
10. Before she got married her last name was Smith, but now her last name is Zephelmacher.

Page 11

457 Hopewood Lane
Cameron, AL 78943-2211
July 8, 2002
Dear Nathan,
I was so glad that you came to visit me. I wish Melissa could have come, but I know she was busy at band camp. I hope she will come next time.

We will probably be in our new house by next August. Our house is at 651 Sunset Drive, so be sure and write me at the new address.

Tell Bobby and Irene that everyone here is thinking of them. They must be having such a wonderful time on their cruise! The only place I ever get to visit is the local zoo. Oh well, it's better than nothing!
Love,
Mark

Page 12 and 13

Answers will vary.

Page 14

February Calendar Page:
Sunday, Wednesday, Friday, Valentine's, Jack's, Boy Scout's

Page 15

9897 Blossom Lane
Peach City, GA 35467-1132
September 12, 2002
Dear Ann,
Yesterday I had to go to the dentist. It was horrible. I had five cavities on each side of my mouth. The dentist said I would have to quit eating chocolate or my head would be full of nothing but fillings. I couldn't help but wonder why they couldn't all be chocolate fillings. Oh well! I will talk to you soon.
Love always,
Carole
223 Mockingbird Street
Allen, TN 38291-2777
October 9, 2003
Dear Aunt Jane,
Hope all is well with you. Things were okay here until you left. We miss you so much. My friends came over yesterday to see you do some more of your lasso tricks, and I told them you had already left for the next rodeo.

Good luck on the circuit. I'll see you the next time you ride into town.
Sincerely,
Sally Mae

Page 16

1. James said, "You are the meanest person I've ever met."
2. Correct
3. Courtney replied, "Someday I'm going to marry him."
4. The teacher said, "If you do not have your homework, you will not have recess."
5. Correct
6. Chloe said, "You better not try to read my diary."
7. Correct
8. Correct
9. "We are all going to campout on Halloween night," Drew explained.
10. "There will be no recess unless everyone sits down and gets quiet," Mrs. Norma stated.

Page 17

Dogwood	blue
Hampton	Year's
December	Shelby
Dear	Canada
Day	wonderful
Saturday	Aunt
Davidson	Shakersville
mall	Love
Doctor	Shelby

Page 18

1. Mr. and Mrs. Boyte are good friends of my parents.
2. At the army base in Kentucky, Captain Jackson accepted only the best from his soldiers.
3. I live in Cannon County in Canton, Ohio.
4. My teacher, Miss Lee, has had a pen pal from Germany since she was in the third grade.
5. We have basketball practice every Tuesday and Thursday night during the months of November, December, and January; however, we don't have to practice on Christmas Day.
6. Coach Binkley said, "If you want to play, you've got to come to each and every practice."
7. When I get older, Doctor Baldwin has promised me I can work at his veterinarian office in Pleasant View.
8. Tristan asked, "Why do I have to clean my room every Sunday?"
9. Cheatham County and Hill County are the two counties left in the football tournament.
10. Monday, Tuesday, Wednesday, Thursday, and Friday are the days we go to school.

Page 19

Answers will vary.

Answer Key (cont.)

Page 20
1. st.
2. Tenn.
3. Mr.
4. M.S.
5. Dr.
6. ave.
7. Wash.
8. J.J.
9. N.Y.
10. U.S.A
11. C.M.S.
12. Fri.
13. Feb.
14. A.M.
15. D.C.

Page 21
1. I am twelve years old.
2. My favorite colors are red, blue, and green.
3. When the sun shines, everyone is happier.
4. All the students went on the field trip.
5. He had five overdue library books.
6–10. Answers will vary.

Page 22
Answers will vary.

Page 23
1. B, That dog just bit me!
2. A, How beautiful you look!
3. A, The house is on fire!
4. A, There's a monster under my bed!
5. B, How exciting it will be to travel in space!
6. B, I loved it!
7. B, I can't believe I get to be the queen!
8. B, There's a terrible wreck just ahead!
9. A, How bright the full moon is!
10. B, She looks absolutely gorgeous!

Page 24
1. C.
2. C
3. X
4. X
5. C
6. X
7. cat's dish
8. dog's treat
9. teacher's desk
10. Kayla Beth's doll
11. horse's oats
12–15 Answers will vary.

Page 25
1. dogs'
2. kids'
3. children's
4. deer's
5. women's
6. toys'
7. geese's
8. hats'
9. sisters'
10. movies'

Page 26
1. C
2. D
3. F
4. J
5. H
6. G
7. A
8. E
9. B
10. I

1. do not
2. have not
3. had not
4. would not
5. she would *or* she had

Page 27
1. At 12:00 midnight the young girl lost her glass slipper.
2. How quickly the time flew!
3. Was there ever a girl more beautiful than she was on that magical, fairy tale night?
4. Why didn't she remember to get home before 12:00 in the morning?
5. The girl's carriage turned into a pumpkin.
6. How lovely everything was before the magic disappeared!
7. Little girls everywhere dream of living in the prince's castle.
8. The girl can't be the prince's bride, unless her feet fit the glass slipper.
9. Life's like a fairy tale; there are good days and there are bad days.
10. Just remember, if you go to a ball, wear a watch that keeps perfect time.

Page 28
1. A
2. A
3. B
4. A
5. B
6. A
7. A
8. B
9. A
10. A

Page 29
Answers will vary.

Page 30
2. February 1, 2003
3. March 1, 2003
4. April 1, 2003
5. May 1, 2003
6. June 1, 2003
7. July 1, 2003
8. August 1, 2003
9. September 1, 2003
10. October 1, 2003
11. November 1, 2003
12. December 1, 2003
13. July 4, 1776
14. April 26, 1955
15. December 28, 1966
16. July 20, 1969
17. March 17, 2002
18. May 15, 1981

Page 31
Answers will vary.
3. 3666 Covington Lane
Chicago, Illinois
89987–1234
6. 342 Meadow View Lane
Sommerset, MA
78965–3221
7. P.O. Box 53
Springfield, Tennessee
8. Dallas, Texas 75526–1234
9. 700 Scoutview Drive
Ashland, Georgia
10. Fairbanks, Alaska

Page 32
Darlington, Maine 78912–0987
January 12, 2002
Dear June,
Always,

Page 33
Richville, Oregon 98761–0223
Novemeber 17, 2003

Dear Sasha,
See you soon,
1. December 15, 1999
2. Dear Mark,
3. Love you a bunch,
4. Sincerely,
5. 345 Oaklawn Drive
Camelot, CA 34571–6767
July 18, 2002

Page 34
1. No, I don't like
2. Yes, I have been to
3. Well, I guess my favorite movie is
4. Why, it's my best friend,
5. Well, I think you are
6. Yes, you can have my
7. No, I don't want to go to
8. Why, I can't believe you think
9. Yes, chocolate is definitely better than
10. No, I will never, ever
11-14. Answers may vary.
11. No, I don't want any frog legs for supper.
12. Well, I've heard some frogs can cause warts.
13. Yes, some frogs are princes in disguise.
14. Why, I don't want any frog legs for supper.

Page 35
1. My favorite meals are breakfast, lunch, and supper.
2. We will attend the meeting at 372 Anderson Lane, Smithville, Kentucky.
3. Yes, you do look like someone I once knew.
4. Well, I would like to go hiking, fishing, and camping.
5. My grandmother is from Nashville, Tennessee.
6. Dear Robert,
Please don't be mad at me. I broke the handle bars on your new bicycle. I will use my allowance to have them repaired. The good news is I only had to get five stitches. The bad news is we can't fix your bike with just a few stitches.
I'm really sorry.
Sincerely,
Irene
7. Please deliver the package to 1789 Grover Drive, Barsdale, Oregon 34567–1299
8. I wish I could take a nap and sleep, sleep, and sleep some more.
9. Yes, I do like ice-cream sodas.
10. Why, I never guessed you like her!
11. The package was addressed to 85 North Michigan Avenue, Louisville, Kentucky, but was delivered to 85 South Michigan Avenue.
12. Well, the last time I saw him he was only three inches tall.
13. Why, performing a play about he world's greatest inventors is a great idea for the drama club, the science club, and the entire school!
14. Dear Sandra,
Please sent me the money you owe me. Cash works nicely, but I will also take a check.
Sincerely,
Teresa
15. You are nice, pretty, and kind.
16. No, I would never tell a lie.
17. Kevin made failing grades on his science, social studies, and math tests.

18. She has taught first grade, second grade, and third grade.
19. Well, that is the funniest thing I've ever seen.
20. No, I won't share my popsicle with you.

Page 36

Benson, Louisiana
Brigham, Louisiana 347
Kingston Place
Benson, Louisiana
December 23, 2002
Dear Betty,
I wanted to write and wish you a happy holiday. I wish we would have some snow over the school break, but since it's hot enough to go swimming, I doubt that will happen. Why, it's hot enough to fry an egg on the sidewalk!
Did you ask your parents for anything special for Christmas? I asked for a camera, some film, and a gerbil. Well, I doubt I'll get the gerbil, but it never hurts to ask.
I will talk to you not Monday, Tuesday, or Wednesday because we will be gone for the fishing trip, but I will definitely call you on Thursday.
Stay cool,
Dewanna

Page 37

1. Jack said, "Yesterday I went to the dentist."
2. "I hate going to the dentist," Marie responded.
3. "It wasn't too bad. I only had one cavity," Jack replied.
4. "Well, when I go, I hope I don't have any cavities," Marie said.
5. Jack answered, "If you brush your teeth regularly you probably won't have any cavities."
6. Marie said, "Of course I brush regularly. I use my favorite toothbrush."
7. Jack responded, "I can't believe you have a favorite toothbrush. What is it?"
8. Marie answered shyly, "Oh, it's nothing. Never mind."

9. Jack said, "You have to tell me what it is. You've made me curious."
10. "Good grief! If you must know, it's a toothbrush shaped like an elephant. I use the long trunk that's filled with bristles to reach my back teeth, and the bristles on the tusks clean my front teeth. That's why my teeth are always pearly white," Marie explained.

Page 38

"I get to go to the concert next week!" Christie exclaimed.
"How did you get tickets?" Brandon asked.
"I won them from a contest on the radio," Christie explained.
"You have to be the luckiest person I've ever met," Brandon said.
"Yes, I am," Christie said with a smile.
Brandon asked, "How many tickets did you win?"
"Two," replied Christie.
"Have you decided who is going with you?" Brandon asked innocently.
"Whoever I invite will have to be someone who is very nice to me," Christie said.
"Of course," Brandon agreed.
"By the way, Christie, do you need any help with your homework?"
"Nice try, Brandon," Christie said.
"What?" Brandon asked innocently.
"I was going to invite you anyway," Christie said.
"Thank goodness," Brandon replied. "I don't even have my own homework finished yet. I didn't know how I was going to help you with yours!"

Page 39

Answers will vary.

Page 40

1. Steve said, "I want to build a treehouse."
2. "Where will you build it?" Sandra asked.
3. "I want to build it in the maple tree in my yard," Steve explained.

4. "Can I help you?" Sandra asked.
5. "Of course you can, but I get to make all the decisions. You are just the helper," Steve said.
6. "Well, if that's the case, I think I'll just build my own treehouse," Sandra answered.
7. "Wait!" Steve exclaimed. "I've changed my mind. You can help make some of the decisions."
8. "You're only saying that because my daddy owns a lumber mill, and you know I can get the wood," Sandra said.
9. "I do need wood to build my treehouse," Steve admitted.
10. "I'll help you," Sandra finally said, "but only if you call me Queen Sandra for the rest of the day."
11. "Good grief!" Steve complained.
12. "Take it or leave it," Sandra responded.
13. "Okay. Okay," Steve agreed. "Let's build that treehouse now, Queen Sandra."
14. "You don't have to bow down when you call me that," Sandra said.
15. "Trust me; I wasn't," Steve said. "I was just tying my shoelace."
16. "A Wonderful Day"
17. "You Are My Life"
18. "The Cat With Three Whiskers"
19. "My Goat, Gabrielle"
20. "The Day No Dogs Would Howl"

Page 41

1–5. Answers will vary.
6. The chapter I like best is "Swimming, Swimming, Swimming," in the book *Summer Vacation*.
7. "She Can Wait" is my favorite song.
8. I read the article, "Getting Better Grades," but I still made a D on my test.
9. My father wrote the hit song, "Daddy Is Great," but he says the words are about his own father.

10. In *Teenager Magazine* the article, "Communicating With Parents," really helped me communicate with my own family.
11. "Snow days are the best school days," Jack said.
12. "I agree with you," Sarah replied.
13. Jack responded, "I wish we could get a snow day soon."
14. Sarah answered, "You know that will never happen. The temperature today reached over one hundred degrees!"
15. Jack sighed and said, "I think I'm going to move to the North Pole."

Page 42

1. C
2. A
3. C
4. A
5. B
6. B
7. A
8. B
9. C
10. A

Page 43

11. C
12. B
13. C
14. B
15. A
16. A
17. B
18. C
19. C
20. B
21. A
22. C
23. C
24. B
25. C
26. C
27. A

Page 44

28. C	33. C
29. A	34. C
30. A	35. A
31. C	36. A
32. B	37. C

Page 45

38. B	41. C
39. A	42. A
40. C	43. C